I0626979

IN THE STRUGGLE

POEMS FROM AN ADDICT'S
HEART TO INSPIRE HOPE

JUSTIN SILVERS

A

PinkShirt Press Publication

In the Struggle

Copyright © 2025 by Justin Silvers

The poems in this collection are based on personal events and true experiences in the author's life. While the events and emotions are factual, some names, locations, and identifying details may have been changed to protect the privacy of individuals.

Published by Justin Silvers/Self-Published

Imprint: PinkShirt Press

First Edition

ISBN: 979-8-218-90037-3

Cover Design: Justin Silvers

Conceptual Design: Joie Wails

Interior Layout: Justin Silvers

Printed in the United States of America

DEDICATION

For My Family

&

To all the beautiful souls who are battling addiction, especially the ones who want to give up because the world has given up on them. The people that don't feel they fit in this life. My heart goes out to you in your struggle. I have been there before. Hopelessness and purposelessness are two things I wouldn't wish on anyone.

May you find hope through my words knowing I have been through my own struggles. I have fought many tough battles, maybe not on the same magnitude or level, but they were sufficient enough to bring me to broken and somehow, I survived. Knowing what I went through and where I am today is proof that anyone can make it out of the darkness.

CONTENT

FOREWORD

In the depths of our struggles, we often discover the most profound voices forged in fire and resilience. It is with honor that I introduce this collection of poetry by Justin. In these pages, you will find a raw and unfiltered expression of his journey through substance use disorder, pain, and ultimately, recovery.

Justin and my brother crossed paths while navigating the challenging landscape of incarceration. It is within those walls that their friendship flourished, and their shared experiences became the foundation for healing. Their connection exemplifies the power of understanding and support, proving that even in the darkest of places, hope can be ignited.

This book is more than a collection of poems; it is a courageous exploration of vulnerability and strength. Justin's words resonate with authenticity, reflecting not only personal battles but also struggles that many face in silence. Through his poetry, he offers a voice to those in similar circumstances, reminding us that we are not alone. This collection invites readers to reflect, empathize, and connect. You will encounter moments of despair, but you will also witness a powerful resurgence.

His poem "Dopamine Is King," inspired by *Dopamine Nation*, delves into the captivating yet challenging nature of desire. In it, Justin explores the internal battles that many endure, revealing how the lure of instant gratification can overshadow the pursuit of long-term recovery. This piece, like the rest of his work, captures the essence of the courage it takes to seek balance amidst the complexities of life.

May this book inspire you, as it has inspired me, to recognize the beauty that can emerge from struggle and to understand that recovery is not just possible; it is a powerful journey worthy of celebration. Justin's writing is a testament to the capacity for change and growth, echoing themes of resilience and the transformative power of self-expression. Your voice matters, Justin, and your courage to share your story will undoubtedly touch many lives.

Maggie Williams, PA-C

PREFACE

I have fought the battle of meth addiction for the last 14 years. I've been incarcerated for 16 out of 41 years of my life. Over the last 10 years I have been locked up every single year during the summer. During this time, I have resolved to figure out my addiction, hitting the books hard and studying why this loser can't win.

It's been a long hard road, but all this wasted, lost time hasn't been for nothing. I have learned volumes about myself, addiction, and life. And I only hope my hard lessons will be absorbed by you, the reader, and you won't have to learn the heart breaking, soul sucking, mind destroying lessons I learned.

These poems are for the addict still struggling in addiction, and the non-addict still struggling with understanding why. I write these words from the heart of my experiences with the sincerest intention of helping to shed light on the darkness that has enveloped my life for so long. And hopefully in the end you feel so not alone. For in fact, I have been in similar shoes, and I see you.

Justin Silvers, Author

IN THE STRUGGLE

LOVING AN ADDICT

Loving an addict must really be tough,
Perhaps we're made of different stuff.
You see my mistakes and the drugs I do,
You don't see me as human too.
I see you as a person going through some things,
You see a scumbag who needs to change.
But I'd give the shirt off my back
and last bit of money,
When you saw me dumpster diving
You thought it was funny.

Did it ever occur that maybe you could help,
Knowing you too have struggled yourself?
I'm not asking for much just take me as I come,
Not having it together doesn't make me a bum.
I'm just trying to figure what life's all about,
Destroying myself I'll figure it out.
I need no help with internal conviction,
All these mistakes fuel my addiction.

But maybe it's time you try on my shoes,

To fight the battle, I always lose.

If you think it's that simple, black and white,

Take my sword and shield, let's see you fight.

When your arms get weak, and knees begin to buckle,

Remember me in the dumpster

and how you chuckled?

It's not so funny when your fighting for your life,

At a gunfight wielding a knife.

So go ahead and tell me how to fix my affliction,

In a place so twisted it sounds like a fiction,

Story of my life was doing so good,

Until I relapsed because I no longer could,

Pretend I had control of my life,

I sold my soul for a hit of the pipe.

I stay up for days or even tweaks,

Go so hard I lost my cheeks.

"Look there's a skeleton on a bike,"

Backpack's on but not to hike.

It contains my life, everything of mine,

Lost in a world where I cannot find.

My way back home, I'm stuck in the mud,
Stomp my boots; thud, thud, thud.
Can't get rid of my dirt, it won't let go,
Only pulls me deeper into this hole.
But when I was younger, I couldn't wait to be older,
Now that I am, I wish it was over.
So, I get high just to feel right
And keep my regrets out of sight.

But I've lost so much time spent in a cell,
Moments of reflection, purgatory or hell?
Down and depressed my life felt over,
With time under my belt, I'm finally sober.

It once was fun but I'm no longer me,
At least not the me I'm wanting to be.
Living this way is no longer fine,
I need some help; do you have some time?
To bring this wreckage back to shore,
But have no doubts, you must be sure.
I'll break your heart, I'll make you cry,
I didn't mean to hurt you, but I had to get high.

It's time for a change, so what do I do?

Keep in mind, I'm not like you.

Been fighting a battle few ever win,

But I won't give up as long as you're in.

I'll stand back up there's still a spark,

It's in the hope you keep at heart.

Now when I see prints in the sand,

I hope there's four as you take my hand.

Or will I walk alone in my shoes,

Because this is a life you said I choose.

Never give up and you will see,

I just needed someone to believe in me.

So lace up your boots, it's about to get rough,

Because loving an addict is really that tough.

CAN'T TRAIN MY DRAGON

Dungeons and dragons, prisons and drugs,
I never believed they could change who I was.
Thought I was stronger than anyone else,
But when I look in the mirror, I don't see myself.
For when I was younger, I thought it was cool,
To chase this dragon after school.
That's how it started from practically nothing,
It took one hit, don't think I'm bluffing.

Back then he was small and could easily hide,
Even snuck him on a carnival ride.
Now he's too big for me to deny,
I can't even cover with one great lie.
So why do I give him so much trust,
When everything he breathes on turns into dust?
I ran so hard to get away,
Tells me he loves me, but I have to stay.
I'm not sure what to do he won't let me go,
It literally feels like I am chained to his toe.
But when I was younger, I got to know him,

Even synced our minds, yet I can't control him.

Thought I did, believed I could win it,

He destroyed my life in under a minute.

All it took was that single hit;

Permanently scarred but totally lit.

It became an obsession, more than a habit,

Like a child with sugar, I just had to have it.

Now I'm back in a dungeon for battling my dragon,

He flies overhead; I can hear him braggin'.

Despite this dungeon he beckons to me,

Lightin' skies on fire 'til he sets me free.

He flies through the clouds like smoke in the wind,

Startin' to wonder if he's really my friend.

I hold on tight, in love with the burn,

When he comes to me, I never pass my turn.

For in my veins, he swims on through,

But more than my breath he takes for true.

When he bites my flesh it feels so right,

Down in this dungeon it's always night.

Still Battling my dragon, stuck in this dungeon,

Unbearable mistakes turned me to plungin',

His dope in my arms, it takes me over,

It's why I relapse every time I'm sober.

It's like everywhere I go these chains I'm draggin',

So, I'm not really confident about training my dragon.

Whenever I make it, he breathes in my face,

Whispering, "come on, you love this taste,"

So, I spat at his fire and ran away,

Still haven't escaped to this very day.

Even stabbed his heart, I thought he was dead,

But we're so intertwined I killed myself instead.

It's like I am him or he is me,

Perpetually condemned, Or will I ever be free?

I didn't defeat my dragon today,

But I won't stop until I can say,

He's up in the stars, now I am free,

I pray there he stays so I can be me.

Been battling so hard to learn how to train him,

But everyone knows you can't train my dragon.

PRESCRIPTION

I haven't been to the top

but familiar is the bottom,

So many scars

can't remember how I got 'em.

I've been locked up and I've been free,

Stood against monsters and I've taken a knee.

I've been in love and I've been cursed,

I've seen the best and dealt with the worst.

I might not be the best person to guide your way,

But this is what I've learned to this very day.

Some die old, some die young,

Whatever the case, try to have fun.

Hold no grudge longer than a count to 10,

That may be the last time you see that person again.

You can save a life with a laugh or a smile,

If someone asks for help, go the extra mile.

Let no moment pass where you can do good,

What if what you did

helped more than anyone could.

It's normal to make mistakes but learn as you go,
In the end, it's the pain that enables us to grow.
Focus on your problems like staring at the sun,
Look for a moment then time to move on.
Stare too long and no one can move you,
For in that moment the pain will consume you.

Never be too good to pull out a woman's seat,
Open doors for little old ladies
and help them cross the street.
Don't ever pass at a chance to love,
But realize it might not always be from above.
Relationships are forged from hardships overcome,
Sometimes your first love isn't always the one.
Love as hard as you can while there is time,
And never, ever be afraid to speak your mind.

Sing and dance like there is no tomorrow,
Music cleanses your soul and shatters the sorrow.
Don't miss the chance to try something new,

If you have a dream, let no one discourage you.

Let no bad choices become your description,

Use them to overcome

and they become your prescription.

Give your best no matter what you do,

Don't take everything to heart,

And always believe in you.

Forgive people often,

Don't forget the past,

Stay a kid at heart,

And try not to grow up too fast.

This isn't the end and the journey's far from done,

So, learn from my mistakes and try to have fun

CONFESSIONS OF A SINNER

Every time I get locked up
it's harder and harder to be here,
I thought repetitions make you stronger,
So why hasn't it gotten any easier?

Every time I come here
it's like a little piece of me leaves you,
Ever tell someone you'd change so much
no one no longer believes you?

I've been so busy weighing dope
I failed to weigh the cost,
Reflections in the mirror
tell me more than weight I lost.
Eyes are windows to the soul
but all the shades are drawn,
Contemplating in my mind, 'when did life go wrong?'
I thought one day I'd prove you wrong,
annihilate your doubt,

Now the walls are closing in, not sure I'll make it out.

Mistakes are catching up to me,

I might be gone awhile,

Such a burden to my soul, can't seem to find a smile.

My darkest hour is upon me

as depression sinks its teeth,

Tears consume my showers

as I struggle with this grief.

Instead of counting sheep,

I'm haunted by bad choices,

Lay awake all damn night listening to the voices.

"Right where you belong" they say

"a reward for your dirt,"

Confessions of a sinner don't seem to help the hurt.

I know it broke your heart

when you heard of all my trouble,

But please don't turn your back,

lest you crush my heart to rubble.

THE VERY NEXT MINUTE

The last time I died it took less than a minute,
All pain was gone, my life was finished.
I broke down a pill I knew what it'd do,
The powder was fine, it's color was blue.
In that minute I only thought of myself,
Couldn't handle regrets, couldn't ask for help.
Dying inside, a life overdue,
Struggling with hope; surrender, I'm through.

I drifted away to a peaceful sleep,
Cheated my life, the price was cheap.
It cost only a minute to chop out a line,
My watch stopped ticking, it ran out of time.
That makes me the bandit who stole me from you,
Decisions so bad, feeling so blue.

I didn't realize the bond my death could rend,
With pain this deep I couldn't pretend.
Not sure what happened, I thought it was over,

Dazed in a hospital, a cop standing over.
Back in the hell I tried to escape,
Couldn't save myself, I lost my cape.

Thought I was super, gave it my all,
The harder I try, the harder I fall.
Heart off-line, I crossed on over,
A shock to my chest; defib controller.
Battling the devil I had no more fight,
Narcan, Narcan a miracle that night.
Alive again, yet far from free,
Became the person I tried not to be.

But I promised to do it, I'd make this time count,
With unbalanced scales I couldn't mount,
Up to the person I swore I would be,
Not legally blind, but why can't I see.
The people who love me no matter my faults,
The struggle inside is not their fault.
I lost my hope in the pit of despair,
Gave up myself, I didn't think they'd care.
But for one minute they thought my life was over,

Hearts ripped from chest; how do I shoulder?
The weight of the world, it's too much for me,
Thought I couldn't do it but now I see.
I don't stand alone, it's not just my fight,
Through their tears and prayers,
I pulled through the night.

It took more than a minute to finally see,
The amazing people God gave me.
The lesson I learned from dying that night,
We all suffer pain, but it'll be alright.
So, cherish the minutes and treasure the past,
For the very next minute might be our last.

AFFLICTION OF HEART

Consistently here for me, in spite of me not,
Miscalculated decisions took what I got.
We all know the story, a lame old excuse,
Gave up my life; I love the abuse.

Embellished achievements squandered to waste,
Blood on my lips; I love how it tastes.
Conviction so deep, repress all my fears,
Confusion in life, the journey's unclear.
Convincingly fair to be stuck on this wheel,
Took my own life, despite how I feel.
Tried to be normal; battle my demons,
With fingers in ears, I muffled their screaming's.

Insufficient endeavors turned crazy in mind,
Seeking the light through darkness, I find.
Absolution the answer, a cure for the curse,
Persistence to better, then go in reverse.
Sent in remission, I thought it was over,

Addiction unconquered; I lost the controller.

A wallowing victim, much pity and sorrow,

Unbroken promises shatter tomorrow.

I fathom to deal, there's surmounting regret,

A subject change helps me forget,

Mistakes that took me so far away,

For corrupted choices, conviction I paid.

With affliction of heart, depression I bleed,

Of forgiveness, I beg, please set me free.

GET BENT

I took a few hits and held them real long,
By the time I exhaled everything was gone.
It seemed so cool like a funhouse mirror,
Now I'm depressed because I'm stuck in here.
The strangest reflections keep staring me down,
Guess I don't need the nose to be a clown.
I locked eyes with a skeleton, he's all in my face,
Keeping me distracted so I'm lost in this place.
He must be my friend because he's always around,
Even picks up my Band-Aids
when they fall to the ground.

The smoke has cleared, everyone's high,
In love with the rush or being this guy?
To suppress regrets I got high alone,
Now I'm in jail and I cry on the phone.
You asked if it's worth it, I said "for sure,"
Looking back now, I no longer concur.
Wish I could hug you, but I'm stuck in this place,

Closing my eyes, all I see is that face.

Tears in your eyes, the judge sent me to prison,

I'm so sorry momma for the way I've been livin'.

Drugs changed who I was; they took me over,

So I know you are happy your baby is sober.

It's not how I imagined it, neither did you,

But I'll see you again when this sentence is through.

I'm no longer surprised how far I can slip,

I lost my footing, but I kept my grip.

I've traveled this path way too long,

To know it's not over, the addiction's not gone.

A moral infraction can take me back over,

Moment by moment I'm keeping my sober.

My mind is clear, the drugs are gone,

If you're not on my team, goodbye so long.

I came a long way from a twacked out junkie,

Put on some weight and got a little chunky.

Now I exhale because my life is content,

And if you want to get high, you can get bent.

HEAVILY BURDENED FRIEND

Oh heavily burdened friend,
Come lend me your ear again.
The weight on my shoulders is astounding,
I can't break free of these sorrows,
It's hard to live for today
when worries consume tomorrow.

Fret not my friend,
I told you, I'd see you through the end.
Waste no worry for what might go wrong,
Rather enjoy the early birds who sing their songs.
While streams erode dirt or pain,
Worries come back down through like rain,
Or perhaps perspectives need new lenses;
A mud-dipped telescope doesn't see so clear,
Peepholes only disclose what is near,
And objects appear closer in certain mirrors,

Yet how do we see the world

through stained glass or eyes,

To protect people from life we fabricate lies

Then adorn masks that conceal such compromise

Acorns expose hearts

through falls that crack their shell,

And dreams come true,

not just through coins wished in a well.

Oh, heavily burdened friend,

Hard times will persist, but I'll go with you the road,

I told you once before, friend, you are not alone.

So pull back your shoulders and lift up your head,

Mourn not for your life but only what is dead.

For clouds may cry unexpectedly

or as predictions told,

But when the sun comes about,

shadows and rain must fold.

INSIDE

Inside this cell, Inside this brain,

Wrapped in chains, I remain.

Letting go of past regrets,

All those times no one forgets.

Reaching up to skies above,

Wonder why I find no love.

Inside this mind, Inside this heart,

Keep myself from falling apart.

As I learn from my past,

No more doubt shall I cast.

Might need help along the way,

Someone to love if I stray.

Will you be there if I call,

Will you laugh when I fall?

Inside this chest, Inside this soul,

As I crawl out of this hole.

Praying for strength in every way,

So many battles everyday.

Will I win or will I fail,

As I climb back up that hill?

Inside this life, Inside this man

Wrought with strength I know I can.

Seeking shelter from the rain,

Trudging on through future pain.

Finally free, no longer bound,

For Inside I am found.

SOBER

I just want to be sober,

So how do I start over?

Time to pass the Controller;

Power button. No pause. Game Over.

The finish lines getting closer,

Addictions force exposure,

These convictions bring me closer,

To your shoulder,

That I might need just to cry on.

Sobriety's driving me,

Something deep inside of me,

Gonna be the best I can be,

So wipe away your tears for me.

All your fears I see,

Afraid you'll bury me before my times come,

But the times come to say that I'm done.

Sick of the run, Sick of the spun,

Sick of the man I've become.

When will I quit? When will I stop?

Does momma have to hear my casket drop?

Tic to the toc, so sick of the clock,

Wish time would stop,

And I gotta skip the walk

around the block where I use to flock,

If I want to stay sober, before my son gets older,

Before my life is over,

So I'm gonna need your shoulder,

Just to cry on.

No more reliving the old days,

Time to abandon my old ways,

Avoiding all the old plays,

"Should've listened," they all say

It's okay to throw the towel in,

It's okay to say that I quit,

It's okay to let go of all the bullshit.

And I know you're still frightened for me,

But I know you're still fightin' for me,

I know you cry hard for me,

because it's hard to see,

This frail version of me.

And you wish I could see your tears for me,

But I wish you could see the hurt inside of me,

Maybe then you'd understand why sobriety

hasn't been easy for me,

But I'm tired of living life through letters,

Tired of wondering if I'll get better,

Tired of standing in this weather, no umbrella,

With so many things I want to tell ya.

So I'm getting sober,

But does addiction have closure?

Emotions overflow like a jam-packed folder,

Tears fall hard as I lose my composure.

Seasons changed and it's getting colder,

Nearly strangers now and quite a bit older,

But thank you for your shoulder,

I'm sober.

And if you ever need a shoulder,

I have two just for you to cry on.

So grateful for you,

The battles aren't through,

But I'm sober.

AN INVISIBLE SET OF CHAINS

My world crumbled as we tore each other apart,
I'll never understand
how we broke each other's hearts.
Maybe we believed the lies
as we took the first hits,
Thought at any moment we could call it quits.
Plunging in deep, a pinch followed by a zing,
Suddenly like puppets dangling by a string.
Darkness without night, a world so gloom,
On a pedestal we held you just for that zoom.

Chase the dragon,
More like shackled to a wagon,
chained and draggin'.
Yeah I got off, fell off, maybe I was nudged,
Now I'm on a new sentence waiting to be judged.
It's not right, it's not fair,
I begged them for help, no one was there.
Thought I was strong, you showed I was weak,
Can't handle the abuse yet turn the other cheek.

Chasing the high while ducking through alleys,
Never imagined this as our reality.
Now here we are with nothing to call our own,
Wiped us out clean and tore apart our home.
Put out on the streets with nowhere to turn,
I wipe away her tears in my heart they burn.
We kept each other warm when no one else would,
Despite all the hardships we try to do good.
As we crash to the bottom,
love and life demand a war,
It's time we fight back harder
than we ever have before.
Starting to think our love gets stronger when it rains,
Perhaps we are bound by an invisible set of chains.

No matter how hard I try
like a scripted life I'm leading,
Sounds a little crazy
but look at the blood I'm bleeding.
Cracked and broken teeth
fill my mouth like a graveyard,
You took everything from me, still became my savior.

Numb to the world, no more pain do I feel,

But through the haze I must stand up and deal.

Look how far I've come, look how far I fell,

An invisible set of chains pulls me back to hell.

Yes, I fell through an abyss without bottom,

See all these bruises, every rung's how I got 'em.

Now here we are torn apart once more,

All I ever wanted was to be how we were before.

Hard lessons learned, don't believe me just look,

Seems I ripped a page right out of God's book.

How'd we get so far from where we once were,

I use to be so positive, now I'm not so sure.

Need to break this cycle,

get out from under this curse,

Seems the harder we battle life only gets worse.

I'm trying to beat this demon,

suck it's venom from our veins,

But it's like we're bound by an invisible set of chains.

YEAH, YEAH

I keep writing these words hoping they come true,

But I keep failing dad, what do I do?

Trying my best to be all that I can,

I want to stand next to you but I'm not half the man.

Your shoes aren't too big

and my feet aren't too small,

But when I wear your shoes, off they fall.

I know you told me life can be rough,

I'm trying Dad I'm just not that tough.

How did you do it, you battled to stop,

Even heard you once out ran a cop.

Then I was born your first boy what a blessing,

You cleaned up your act

will you teach me this lesson?

Arms to the sky, filled with joy,

It was me, Dad, your first baby boy.

With great expectations you raised a man,

Who could take on the world with just his hands.

You're always there for me truly a great father,

But I keep messing up, Dad, why do you bother?

I've been living all wrong

doing nothing you showed me,

But I'm breaking these chains

so they no longer hold me.

Because everything you taught I alluded to evil,

But I wrote the script so here comes my sequel.

"Get your head out of your ass,"

your words are sincere,

You never walked away

and you're still right here.

Because I am your buddy and you are my Dad,

You taught me the boring life isn't so bad.

Back then you were my hero and still are today,

I love you, Dad, is not all I can say.

I thank God for giving me a father like you,

And "Yeah, Yeah" means I love you too

BAND-AIDS

I Have chosen paths without much reason,
My life melted away like the change of a season.
In the glistening moments of my awakening
I reckoned to a path and wandered far astray,
Lost in the abyss of moments gone wrong
wondering if this was my last day.

Sinking down deep, below the unknown,
Traveling to a place I found myself all alone.
Days submerged into a suffocating struggle
I thought wouldn't last,
Now here I am putting Band-Aids on my past.

The snow globe of my life was shaken
and turned around,
Starting to see clearly as debris hits the ground.
Negative voices keep telling me what I'm not,
I look in the mirror and realize what I've got.
Inadvertently finding myself addicted

to a moment I could no longer resist,
In the end I realized it was you that I miss.

I wake up every morning to see your face,
Sad to touch you, there's a picture in your place.
It broke my heart when they took me away,
I'll fight with my life to get back to you someday.

No more feeling sorry for myself,
No more standing around,
This time I'll build my life back up,
As the Band-Aids fall to the ground.

IT AIN'T OVER 'TIL IT'S OVER

Spiraling out of control, can't help myself,
Destroying my life I'm Wreck-It-Ralph.
The snowball effect has taken over,
Crumbling the life I built while sober.

I tell you I'm fine with a frown on my face,
Smile suppressed, I'm full of disgrace.
You think I'm a failure, I believe it too,
Despite all the hardships I made it through.

But this lie isn't mine, addiction took over,
Now every day's a struggle to keep the controller.
You think of my life as fun and carefree,
But most of the time I even scare me.
I'm talking to shadows, they seem so real,
Sometimes I think they even know how I feel.
And I've cried so intensely you wouldn't believe,
I wasn't going to a funeral or trying to grieve.
Body convulsing as tears hit the floor,

Everything's gone, I can't lose anymore.
Perhaps I was grieving because I had died,
The person I was is no longer inside.

I screw over family and anyone who cares,
Then find myself wondering why no one is there.
Like Adam Sandler in the movie "Click",
Fast Forward my life so I don't have to forget,
All the pain and regrets my decisions brought,
Because these drugs are more powerful
than I ever thought.

On cloud nine I've done the unthinkable,
Like Titanic thought I was unsinkable.
But I'm flooded with mistakes, soon I'll be under,
A storm's rolling in I can hear the thunder.
It's getting so close can feel it in my knees,
I need your help, please, oh please,
Give me your hand, I need you to still care,
Pulling you under I know it's not fair.
I've been so consumed with chasing the high,
It's not just the bad moments that pass me by.

Morals are twisted and tied in a knot,

Trying to be someone I know I am not.

I missed Grandma's birthday,

my son just turned eight,

The world keeps spinning, life does not wait.

Absent from funerals, even my sisters wedding,

And there's so much more I keep regretting.

Holidays with family and game night fun,

All given up because I was too spun.

Walking with Mom or working with Dad,

One day they'll be gone and will I have had,

Made them proud to call me their son,

Or will I be high and still on the run?

But the snowballs are melting,

and Ralph's getting tired,

I sent him on home, his ass is fired.

Because it's time to rebuild and get back to sober,

As someone once said, "it ain't over til it's over".

RUNNING OUT OF TIME

My four year old is about to turn eight,
I lost all those years fighting my fate.
Supposed to be a father, I got high instead,
Chasing after shadows in the land of the dead.
It sure wasn't worth it, not even a bit,
But I love that stuff way more than I admit.

Like sinking in quicksand trying to break free,
The more I struggle the more I see.
I'm in over my head just about to tap,
When my four year old appears on my lap.
Arms around my neck he gives me some hugs,
"I need you, Dad, please get off the drugs."
He's crying and shaking, trembling at the knees,
I squeeze him tighter, "son please don't leave."
When I realize I'm hugging myself I cry even more,
My stomach hurts so bad, I fall to the floor.

Then I recall his words and his tears on my face,
Not sure of the time and there's none left to waste.
So I pull myself to my feet with hands on the sink,
Splash water on my face and take a long drink.

I dry my face and shake off all the remaining sand,
When I'm confronted in the mirror
by a strung out looking man.
Somehow he reminds me of someone I used to know,
And when I look him deep in the eyes
my fears only grow.

Suddenly I realize this stranger is me,
In denial awhile now, it took too long to see.
I don't want this curse anymore,
someone please take it,
Without my son in my life I know I won't make it.
He's getting much older, not sure if he still needs me,
I have to believe he does,
it's the only thing that frees me.
But if he saw me like this it would tear him apart,
A skeleton can't be a father, he doesn't have a heart.

But I do have a heart, and it beats just for him,

I pray for strength every day,

Oh, please God, Amen.

One day I'll hold him in my arms,

one day I'll get him back,

I'm sick of hugging these photographs,

they don't hug me back.

And even though I'm getting stronger,

I still can't say I'm fine,

For sands fall through the hourglass

and I'm running out of time.

DOPAMINE IS KING

I've been given a curse doctors deem a disease,
You call it my crutch and do not believe.
Your doubt doesn't make it any less true,
Of course I got high because I chose to.

But now I'm addicted and don't know why,
Naïve and gullible I fell for a lie.
Believed I could stop after every hit,
Strung out for days, why can't I quit?
I dove in the pool sure I could swim,
No knowledge of depth or what I was in.

So maybe there's a lesson I ain't been hearin',
You're missin' one too, so lend me your ear and,
I'll tell you what I've learned about addiction,
First open your heart and have some conviction.

I don't have a Ph.D. or a fancy plaque,
Experience is my Professor

so please don't turn your back,

But I graduated with honors

from the school of hard knocks,

Sitting at the table with murderers and card sharks.

I'm known as a docket number and judged by my tats,

They don't know who I am or care for the facts.

Classified as a criminal because I'm addicted,

High-five in the courtroom,

another druggie convicted.

But we're all addicted to the exact same thing,

You think I'm crazy but look at the brain.

Dopamine is a chemical that says we need more,

A reward chemical with a double-edged sword.

You get it from sugar and social media the same,

Even gambling releases Dopamine in the brain.

Too much Dopamine causes psychosis,

Something like a caterpillar

going through metamorphosis.

Instead of a butterfly you become a monster,

Wake up in jail with your name on the roster.

If you're lacking Dopamine you'll soon be depressed,

You won't care to eat, drink, or even have sex.

In fact you'll die from a lack of desire,

But excessive Dopamine will get your mind wired.

It'll have you like a puppet, manipulate you for more,

The difference in my drug is it releases way more.

If shopping released as much Dopamine as Meth,

I'm convinced we'd shop ourselves to death.

Yet addicts are treated like common crooks,

Because we are judged like mislabeled books.

But it's time to unmask and adorn who we are,

Put the lies on the floor, could we take it that far?

And prescribe better medicine for battling addiction,

Because disease isn't cured with a criminal conviction.

And even if doing drugs really isn't your thing,

Make no mistakes, Dopamine is king.

FIREPROOF

Getting stronger, looking higher,
Forge with persistency, feet are on fire.
You can hit me, maybe even drop me,
Don't get in the way, no one can stop me.

I studied your moves, I know what you're about
I got what it takes, I'm crashing you out.
There's no more excuses; extinguished them all.
Give it my life, succeed or fall.

Yes, I'll admit I've been a liar,
Said I was fireproof, now I'm on fire.
You burnt me once, burnt me twice,
Hurt so bad I took my life.
Surrendered to you, I thought it was over,
Buried in dirt up to my shoulders,

But I'm fighting back, taking my freedom,
Can no longer join 'em so now I'll beat 'em.

You created a monster messing with me,

Don't have to believe but promise you'll see.

I'm done being the thief who stole his own life;

I watched it dissipate like mist in the night.

I vomit regrets and so many mistakes,

Getting better, still got the shakes.

It's not from withdrawal, I'm just scared,

If I fail this time you won't think I cared.

That's not the case for I always have,

It's just hard to get off this distorted path.

But I don't want you at my funeral

hating me for leaving,

So I'm changing my life; there'll be no more grieving.

Refining these thoughts, only actions show true,

The intentions of my heart, I'm coming home to you.

My demons took me to an endless abyss,

They had me distracted but it's you I miss.

So I'm going to the top and only looking back,

To remember where I'm from, not where I lack.

Said it so often words lack meaning,

My life's a mess, it's time for a cleaning.

So I'm weeding them out; all the negative people,

Can't contemplate life stuck in this peephole.

Standing alert, eyes on horizons

Strategic moves, no compromising.

I won't do it no more, I can't fail again,

An Olympic medalist; trained to win.

But I figured it out,

I'm ready for this.

Hard lessons learned

Class dismissed.

THE BEAUTY OF NOW

Tomorrow will be better, tomorrow there'll be more,
Tomorrow's the moment we've been waiting for.
We neglect today, we never live in the moment,
The past is present, we can't let go of it.

We miss out on life and the beauty of now,
We can't be happy, we don't know how.
But what if we treasure the moment we're in,
Treat every moment as a very best friend.
The past might hurt, tomorrow might be better,
But today is a present now and forever.

Every day is wrapped in its very own way,
So why not cherish the moments of today?
Some days will be bad, some days will be great,
Let's enjoy this day, we best not wait.

This is the secret to a happy life,
To live in the moment every day and night.

The past is behind us, tomorrow hasn't arrived,

So today let's be grateful, grateful we're alive.

For we can be happy, we can learn how,

If we live in the moment and the beauty of now.

BETTER WEATHER

I'll never forget your voice
when you caught me in the shed,
I'll always remember your tears
and the words you had said.
"What are you doing,"
you cried at the needle in my arm,
How could I be so careless
and cause you so much harm.
Dad didn't see this, but he was there,
And I know it affected him more than was fair.

Not sure how to forgive myself for what you saw.
Only wish I could take that memory
and put it in a jar,
Bury it deep, forget it existed,
Looking back now, I should have resisted.

I heard your hearts shatter as I tried to cover it up,
This isn't what it's supposed to mean,

your little boy's all grown up.

I'll never forget that day, neither will you,

Just know yours weren't the only hearts broken in two.

There's one more thing you must know above all,

It wasn't on you to prevent my fall.

It's not your fault I turned out this way,

I chose this path and decided to stray.

I know I haven't been more than a zero,

Just know you've always been my heroes.

You taught me to work hard, how to be a man,

And to fight for my family with all that I am.

I have no excuse, not a single right,

I let addiction consume me

and eventually take my sight.

But I am fighting to get better, I'm not walking away,

Anticipate the moment when you will say,

I've become the man I was meant to be,

And the time has arrived that you are proud of me.

You saw me at my worst, a skeleton at best,

But your love never faltered, never went to rest,

So I'm picking up the pieces,

getting my life together,

For when the storm clears

I promise there's better weather.

NO TOMORROW

Tears fill my eyes blurring these words on paper,

We lost so much time together, vanished like vapor.

Wrinkles on your face say I've been gone too long,

I'm trying to do right

but everything turns out so wrong.

Made so many mistakes it's hard to keep hope,

But shadows and dust remain if I can't learn to cope.

Sure can't fly, and I'm so afraid to fall,

Lost so many battles, can't afford to lose them all.

But everything vanishes if I don't follow,

Life ceases to exist when death does swallow.

The pressure is mounting, make no mistakes,

Everyone's watching, can't control the shakes.

Ten point zero etched on a scale,

My life in shambles if I do fail.

This is my shot, my final one,

But nothing is finished until it's done.

There is no joy, so much sorrow,

If I don't win there is no tomorrow.

I won't let you down, no not this time,

Fight for this life, or forfeit mine.

RIPPLE EFFECTS

Monsters in our mind whisper,

Destruction's been administered.

Stars wonder why asteroids cry,

While tears shoot across a deep blue sky,

Wrinkling oceans,

with shockwaves and potions.

Fears set on the horizon,

But inside keep on rising.

Tears burn, eyes sting,

Secrets, not surprising.

Ripple effects, domino's crash,

Wonder why babies laugh.

Planes fly, take the night,

Lightning strikes, lost the fight.

Thunder rumbles in our mind,

Made mistakes, press rewind.

So unsure, but I'll find,

What it takes to get what's mine.

DEAR BROTHER

It's been too long since we last saw each other,
What's with this nonsense, man, let's get together.
I love hanging with you, it's always so great,
Life's too short we best not wait.

We'll cruise the town, jam some music,
Even hit 90 in Mom's new Buick.
Smoke golf balls into the farmer's field,
Go so long our arms must yield.

Building big bon-fires, our family gets down,
Come at us, they better ask around.
You don't play when it's family, neither do I,
But both had our share in making them cry.

Float down the river, we have so much fun,
Party all day 'til we extinguish the sun.
Nobody makes Jell-O shots stronger than you,
Fire up the grill, you're good at that too.

Yesterday we were throwing rocks at each other,

Today we are older and I miss my brother.

Life is too short to keep staying away,

We're family, bro, don't stray away.

Be my best friend, I'll invite you over,

Maybe you can help me stay sober.

Now we are older, I'm so proud of you,

You changed your life and now look at you.

But never forget

who was there in your darkened days,

You found true love and I hope that it stays.

No matter where life takes you,

you have a family here,

"We Love You Bro," do I make myself clear?

Look at my life, how long I've been gone,

I miss my family, you know I was wrong.

I'm not telling you to change,

just keep the family focus,

Don't be like me and do everyone bogus.

It's weird I'm trying to be more like you,

But you're my little brother,

And I think you're pretty cool.

"What up Ninja," we say on the phone,

True we're adults, I didn't say we're both grown.

We're in touch with the kids who live in our hearts,

We laugh and run when we hear Dad's farts

All joking aside, I Love You Man,

Let's load up on BB's and shoot down some cans.

ONE MINUTE

Never underestimate the impact of one minute..

Give it my all, true love unconditionally
Should make a difference.
Family functions, reunions, weddings, funerals;
You're never here.

One minute, I used to believe you could change.
Missing so much– all of our lives– your own life.
When will it be enough?
One minute without the luck,
One minute you don't come back ever.
Days go by so fast... Missed family photographs,
Trying to get one in before you slip away again.

Saw a girl tweaking at a concert,
A song about sobriety,
Tasha and I locked eyes.
We hugged and cried thinking about our brother.

Hard to see addicts tweaking,
Can't help but watch them.
I get sad; somewhere people are looking at you,
Laughing at you, scared of you, sorry for you.

Found you freezing cold in a dumpster.
You don't ever want to picture
someone you love like that,
Not for one minute.

Talk, cry, hug at mom and dad's,
Trying to shake the image,
I took your picture that day,
Hoped you'd never want to be like that again,
Even for one minute.

My heart broke.
It wasn't the end,

You sat there looking like a 70 year old man,
Life and love gone. Eyes sunken in,
Pale, face wrinkled, skin and bones,

Dirty, smelly, missing a shoe,

A shell of a person who is supposed to be my brother.

I begged you not to get out.

You turned and gave me the smallest smile,

For one minute I thought about kidnapping you.

We all loved you.

"You don't have to live like this,"

You said "I know," and got out,

Tears in your eyes.

When will you not quit on us?

In one minute...

You unpacked your whole life from my car,

40 years draped over your back,

Dropped off at a druggie hotel.

I didn't want anyone to see my car there.

I cried the whole way home,

It may have been the last time I saw you.

That little smile.

Quickly I left.

Didn't want you to see my tears,

Tears of hurt, tears of not understanding.

Confused and frustrated,

What's right? What's wrong?

Did I fail as a sis?

Would it have made a difference

If I would have spoken up for one minute?

Our name plastered in the paper

On Facebook,

Attached to drugs and crime.

Embarrassing.

Finally a jail call;

Sure beats messages of overdose, of suicide...

Happy for one minute–

No longer homeless, starving or dead.

Next minute.....

Heart dropped;

Super 8 hotel...

Overdose...

Too shaken to drive,

Dead or alive?

So called friends left you

Not knowing the outcome.

You slept for days,

Mom and Dad watched over you all night.

Can't imagine how it breaks them,

Our parents-

To watch you go through this.

To never be able to reach you.

After coming down you took off.

The terms of your decisions.

When will you not quit on us?

"Mom, what, he's dead?"

You wanted to end your life.

You stopped breathing,

I truly thought it was the end.

Mom lost it when they told her,

Her baby's heart stopped.

She couldn't bear it,

Like someone ripped out her heart.

Did we fail? Did we enable?

Why don't you want to be around us?

Why won't you fight for us?

Homeless, on the streets, starving.

Are we so terrible you'd rather?

"Mom, what, he's dead?"

You've never heard anyone cry or scream

As hard as I was in that minute.

I heard mom's voice,

"No, I said he's alive….. it's not good,"

Overdose. Meth. Heroin. Fentanyl.

A handful of pills.

"He's a good kid,"

The officer wouldn't let him die,

Narcan, Narcan, Defib.

Heart back online.

Straight to Facebook,

"Please pray for my son,

Fighting for his life,"

One minute at a time.

COVID restrictions,

Can't be there.

Calls came in.

"What's going on?" She's crying too hard.

Her baby's heart stopped,

"Please just pray."

Prayers answered;

Moved to ICU,

Might still overdose again.

"Keep praying."

That was the hardest night.

You didn't come see any of us.

We almost lost you.

We didn't hear from you for days.

I felt sorrow and depressed,

Your life must be so bad,

That was your only way out.

Back to being pissed;

Why couldn't you reach out to us for help?

When will you not quit on us?

Became numb over the years,

Put memories to the back of our minds,

Worry every day if you're alive.

Every minute.

Her baby's heart stopped.

She lost it.

We always did stuff as a family;

Pool parties, canoeing, tubing, family reunions,

We always look for you,

You're never there.

Got used to never seeing you.

Dad with tears in his eyes.

Dad never cries.

Forgiveness and letting go.

Must bury these moments.

Blood pressure through the roof.

We love you.

Don't get upset,

You need to know these things,

Mom's getting sick.

Can't imagine how you'd feel if....

But one minute...

You are going to be off on a high or in jail,

And one minute,

Somebody won't be here when you get back.

I may have just seen you for the last time.

At one point you turned

And gave me the smallest smile.

One minute enjoying a peaceful night.

The next minute your heart stopped.

And for one minute

I experienced the most heart wrenching pain.

One minute my world turned upside down,

For one minute you were gone forever...

Luckily it was only one minute,
One minute I never want to feel again.
A pain so deep
You know your life would have been changed forever.
The kind of pain that leaves an emptiness
In your heart that never goes away.

One minute you're here,
One minute you're healthy,
One minute you're high,
One minute might be your last.
We're tired and exhausted.
Make up your mind.
One minute is all it takes,
One minute is all that's left.
What will you do with one minute?
Make the next minute count....

"Mom, what, he's dead?"

Luckily, this time it was only one minute.

One minute I never want to feel again.

Not even for one minute.

HEROES DON'T CRY

I've been calculating the strides it takes to be a hero,
Underdog upward punch, coming from zero.
They say courage is not a lack of fear,
Even the bravest suppress many tears.
And that should make me feel better,
But honestly, I'm more scared now than ever.

This beat down path still wears me out,
So deep in the thicket not sure there's an out.
I can't go backwards there's too many dangers,
If I stay still nothing ever really changes.
So I step forward despite my trepidation,
So much time expired there's zero left for wastin'.
For darkness encroaches
sneaking the light from my skies,
But a miracle born put a twinkle in my eyes.
Lost all control I can't help but to cry,

Wait, heroes don't cry, do they?

I recall a flashback,

With memories of map gas

Bellowing out of a tank,

There was no time to think.

Dad yelled "there's gas,"

Instincts acted fast,

Can in hand,

I clutched and ran.

I knew not to stop, even after I was dropped,

By an explosion that sent me flying,

My dad could be dying, there's no time for crying,

I sent to the canister goodbye, and.

Went back in the smoke,

Despite that I choked.

I found my father and extinguished the flames,

If not for my actions life wouldn't be the same.

My sister spoke through held back tears,

But her words came out clear though,

"Justin, You're a hero".

Dad's hands and face suffered third degree burns,

But home from the hospital, a grateful return.

I guess not heroes have time for a cape,

If one is required I'll fashion a drape.

But what if I do have what it takes,

And what if I try yet everything still breaks,

Do I cut on my heart to purge my mistakes.

To prove my intentions were meant for your good,

To wipe away your tears like a real father should?

I know actions speak louder when they fly at fruition,

The fate of a shooting star starts at the wishing,

And it's hard to be a hero when presence is missing,

Or to plot a course if you know not the mission.

Releasing my grip nearly brought my destruction,

Oblivious your absence could cause this dysfunction.

Yet I fight for my boys day after day,

Still struggling to keep the demons at bay.

All fears manifested when they showed me your tears,

Whispering true lies into your ears.

"Your father doesn't love you because he's not here,"

But I am still here, still alive, still believing,

Hold off on the grieving,

I'm done fighting when I'm done breathing.

Even then I won't quit,

My only regret

Was ever letting you go,

For eternity I'll show,

There's no place I can go,

Where my heart and my soul,

Aren't left with a hole,

Because you're not here by my side.

So many tears I have cried,

I promise they lied.

For I never not loved you so much,

On their words they will munch,

For one day we'll touch,

And you'll know my love was true.

I paid all my dues, now I'm coming for you,

I promise it's true.

Your tears are what kept me alive.

It all comes with the price,

So I'll give my own life.

But I cannot pretend,

Your heart broke and then,

Mine didn't shatter to pieces.

That is a lie, for every night I still cry,

I try, and I try, and I try.

Because a son with no father,

is a jungle without water,

A heart bent on falter,

Brought my knees to the altar.

Pleading for mercy over and over,

But it'll only be over once you're back in my life,

I've sharpened my knife,

Also my mind,

So one day they'll find,

The story of a father who refused to surrender.

I hope the light in your eyes

merely fades but not dies, remember,

The sun sometimes hides

behind the clouds of the storms,

Yet everyday we look up our faith is restored.

For winds blow the clouds until they are gone,

See, the sun never left it was there all along.

So next time those demons insist on deceiving,

Please consider the facts,
And hold tightly to hope, because Dad's coming back.

They say heroes don't cry
but I most certainly do,
And with or without a cape
I hope I'm a hero to you.

MISSING YOUR WORRY

I feel like a burden when you pick up my slack,
You tell me you love me you got my back.
I'm not at home perhaps this is best,
Hang up your worries get some rest.
Your prayers were answered I called from jail,
Happy I'm safe, no-bond bail.

Now here I sit missing your worry,
You're not in here no need to hurry.
I'm definitely safe but far from okay,
A second's an hour an hour's a day.
Forgotten and alone in this desolate place,
At least out there I had a space.
A car from my home not truly ideal,
A semblance of comfort behind that wheel.
Somewhere to go when I had nowhere else,
I could cruise with the homies or chill by myself.

So how is it better to feel this alone,

Begging for attention strung out on a phone?

Listening intently I hope for a chime,

Everyone's so busy can't find the time.

I try to be patient, I know the day is coming,

Announce my release, no one comes running.

But they said I matter, I believe what they told me,

Clutching covers so tightly, there's no one to hold me.

More important I felt at my bottom and hopeless,

Feigning for attention nobody notices.

But when I was homeless,

hungry, doped and depressed,

I lived for your messages they were the best.

"You got this," "we love you," "you're not alone,"

Those messages that saved me, I saved to my phone.

Deep in my heart I buried them too,

In my darkest moments they carried me through.

Now that I'm here I get hardly a word,

Karmatic justice perhaps is deserved.

But do I have to be falling or lying in dirt,

For someone to notice this loneliness hurts?

In your mind you think I'm better off here,

But you don't see my pain or the quantity of tears,

That flow on the drain hidden from sight,

Sometimes I cry in the middle of the night.

Because I'd rather my funeral with hearts full of hurt,

Then stacking on time like shovels of dirt.

And being forgotten because of this place,

Do you not know you put a smile on my face,

By answering my calls, or saying a prayer,

You really won't enable me, I promise, I swear.

Mind bending demons are hard to avoid,

When you open your heart to a massive void.

So hand or shoulder is certainly essential,

Going it alone is breaking my mental.

What I need is your attention

it's not about being safe,

It's knowing I matter and your heart has a space.

To believe in me whenever I fall,

And send some money so I have it to call.

My greatest hope is to manifest my wish,

Of knowing my presence has really been missed.

And a little of your time is more than enough,

To help me feel better and get through some stuff.

As it doesn't take much to fill a heart,

"I miss you so much" is a great place to start.

Because missing your worry has gotten me all worried,

I'm not even dead but it feels like I'm buried.

THE FIRST REASON I SMILED

Blessed with a gift since day and my birth,
Come darkness or light you made my life worth,
The heartaches and struggles
I barely scraped through,
Encouraging words, "Mom, thank you."

"For standing so strong through all of these years,
And giving me love despite all the tears,
You shed for me like sad days of rain,
I broke your heart to fill it with pain.
With these storms I brought, came undue fright,
You worried for me night after night.
Would I come home or back to a cell,
You stayed by my side come heaven or hell.
Yet in the face of disgrace and pain I bring,
You answer my calls whenever they ring.
Reminiscing our days I think of your laugh,
Those are the moments that help me get passed,
Feeling my heart has been stabbed with a knife,

For missing so much of your beautiful life.

When I came to this world crying and cold,

Tear ducts filling as emotions explode,

Wrapped in a blanket, held to your chest,

I knew right then you were the best.

Your comfort's embedded deep in my soul,

Thank you, Ma, for not letting go.

And being amazing from the start,

I love you so much with all of my heart.

And I promise this now, there's no mother like mine,

Your hugs bring me home and settle my mind.

That no bond is greater than mother and child,

You are after all the first reason I smiled."

TELL ME

Tell me you need me, then say I can't stay,
Tell me it hurt you to push me away.
Tell me come home I'll give it my best,
Tell me it's okay I made this big mess.

Tell me I'm beautiful, don't treat me so ugly,
Tell me you're waiting to kiss me and hug me.
Tell me you got me or turn and walk away,
Tell me someone heard all the times that I pray!

Tell me I'm worth it, I forget that I am,
Tell me mistakes don't define who I am.
Tell me you're proud, say it like you mean it,
Tell me you love me, I'm telling you I need it.

Tell me something good or lie to my face,
Tell me your eyes won't judge my disgrace.
Tell me I'm normal, let's pretend that I am,
Tell me it don't matter, you're here till the end.

Tell me you hear me, at least say something,

Or tell me, tell me, tell me I'm nothing!

CONDITIONS

At a juncture in life to lay it down or take a stand,
Done letting mistakes define who I am.
But promises left broken breed rejection,
And made-up minds inhibit correction.
Still determined to change
though everyone's forgetting,
I keep falling down but I also keep getting,
Back up to try again it's only over when I don't,
You say I can make it but you think that I won't.

Where did unconditional love find all its conditions?
Tell me I'm wrong but I remember just wishin',
I never got booted due to my addiction,
At least at home I strived for remission,
Once foot hit curb I lost all conviction,
Blast off to the sky no more resistin'.

Now the lifestyle took ahold of me,
What could I do or revert to the old me,

Before the trying and the poetry,

After the courts had their go with me.

Demon self-invited to the feast,

Life extols another piece,

Racking up charges to escape the police.

So make your conjecture but leave room for facts,

No one was there when my life went off tracks.

They call it tough love,

But it's more like the glove,

Of a midget worn by a giant.

Label me defiant,

Because I'll never stop tryin'.

Yet I promised myself to now let them know,

It broke my heart I had nowhere to go.

Surfing trap couches to feel not alone,

Just down the street but so far from home.

So what would you do if you knew nothing else?

Tell me you love me yet fend for myself.

I'm a piece of a puzzle in the wrong place,

Angels and demons they both know my face.

Now darkness endeavors to devour my soul,

In a downward spiral I'm out of control.

But you're not your mistake neither am I,
Say you won't judge me but eyes they lie.
My mountains of dirt I leveled with time,
And paid in full my debt to crime.
With no more to pay I'm done with the lesson,
Cross fingers and pray a sinner's confession.

But it's time to check her hearts as often as a phone,
No one in this life should ever feel alone.
Never deprive someone of their purpose,
It only convinces demons to surface.
For true love stipulates not if or when,
Is solid to the core ride or die to the end.
Standing by your side clutching to your waist,
Laughing hysterically in trouble face.
So if you're going to have my back
you better have heart,
Even shadows abandoning me whenever it's dark.
Maybe then we can remove the conditions,
If you're willing to accept me no matter my condition.

Sequester your judgments

not every mistake is a crime,

We are all humans for the very first time.

And we can go our separate ways

because of bad weather,

Or we can learn to dance in life storms together,

Mending broken promises to settle your mind,

But only if we leave the conditions behind.

TO MY MONSTER WHO NEVER SLEEPS

I have a little dark place deep in my heart,
It's where I find myself when the bullshit starts.
It made me regret all the things I had done,
Even living another day under the sun.
But I became who I am forged in that place,
It's where I found the strength to wear my own face.

So I'm not sorry that I broke your heart,
Or sorry that I let you down,
I discovered who I was not having you around.

I'm not sorry for the mistakes,
Or uncalculated risk,
I needed it all to happen to notice what to miss.

I'm not sorry that I fell again,
Or how it wrecked me,
I needed to be destroyed to let my pain direct me.

So don't you dare feel sorry for me,

Don't you even shed a tear,

I'm climbing up this mountain

There's nothing left to fear.

I've fallen more than a dozen times

I'm conditioned just for this,

So dry your eyes just for me

It's time for you to miss.

Wondering if I'm alive or dead

A skeleton on a buzz,

I was destroyed by a monster

But never again because,

My soul's been set on fire

I won't revert to that version,

When I wasn't quite a monster

Yet not exactly a person.

In my hands I wield sobriety, on my way to slay you,

Not at all sorry I must betray you.

It never bothered you to say things like,

"Trust me, I can save you."

You left me in my dirt abandoned and small,

Convincing everyone I would surely fall.

Those are the times you swore you'd have my back,

When I looked around

you were there and that's a fact.

Then one day it clicked

Why you were always around,

You only lived to see me plummet to the ground.

You prayed for my downfall

most patiently you waited,

when my life turned to crap

You fed me what I hated.

I took it in strides your comfort became my home,

In that darkness you left me desperate and alone.

But I don't regret our journey

I'll never forget the feeling,

Of saying endless prayers

that never breach the ceiling.

And I will never forget our time

the darkest days of past,

It's time to let you go

you stole my life so fast.

In the blink of an eye
41 years swirled down the drain,
I saw my name in the dictionary
The definition read "insane".

So I'm not sorry that I broke your heart
no tears will be shed,
Not while you're hoping and wishing
today I was be dead.
I caught your scheme at the bottom
that time I tried to die,
My insurmountable regrets
I couldn't stop getting high.

Then I found some courage
In my time away from humanity,
To rewrite my own life
and redefine my insanity
I was crazy in my addiction
Now I'm crazy for recovery,
Incited by my corner shouting that they love me.

Now that my mind's been restored,

I'm coming for you,

You see the mob behind me,

Yeah they're coming too.

So get ready for this battle

Death is at your door,

Because I finally realized, Addiction

I don't need you anymore.

I'm not sorry that I broke your heart

Not sorry that I let you down,

It's time I step away

For something better I have found.

That dark place in my heart I transformed into light,

And to my monster who never sleeps

I finally say goodnight.

ROULETTE ADDICTION

Methamphetamine rush,

Just did way too much.

Hush, what's that I hear,

My rapid heartbeats or the feds growing near?

Damn, now I'm flying through the sky,

Astronaut people have never been so high.

And I never want to come down,

Police in pursuit of a strung-out clown.

I can't remember to eat,

Lost 40 pounds in over a week.

Face sunken in can't find no sleep.

But still looking good; I'm stuck in the mirror,

Shadow people creep, they whisper in my ear...

So strung out it's hard to forget me,

Red team, Blue team

Someone's out to get me.

Quick kill the lights,

Peeking out the windows, think we're out of sight.

Staring at cameras, so damn tweaked,

Freaking out now, front door creaked.

Hearts racing, haven't moved for hours,

How many days can we go without showers.

Holding in breathes, think they can hear,

Every single heartbeat, they keep growing near.

Keys jingle. A whispered sound,

Hiding in an attic, wish to be found.

Sweating my ass off, totally worth it,

Dental hygiene's far from perfect.

Not sure how I'm surviving,

Now this shit's got me dumpster diving.

Been up for over a week,

Everything I find I gotta keep.

Knives, tapes, flashlights, glue,

And don't forget backpacks too…

Coming down soon, time to eat,

But got nowhere safe to rest my feet.

Close my eyes just for a minute,

Backpacks gone and all that was in it.

My whole life was in that pack,

Plot revenge, never get it back.

Nothing left, find some rest,

Hope I wake up not so depressed...

Time to get up, let the cycle resume,

Wish my name was on the face of a tomb.

So many messages left unchecked,

But only loved ones do I neglect.

I hate this shit so damn much,

It literally ruins everything I touch.

So why do I keep living this way?

Roulette addiction, forced to play.

But forget this life,

I'm dropping the pack,

Time to take my own life back.

OVERCOME

Agony of the past echoes in my mind,
Stirs overwhelming sensations
I thought I left behind.
Shreds of my heart
vaporized by bitter words unspoken,
But a new hope and strength arise,
And I've found a way of coping.
Saying goodbye to bad endings
And awakening to a new start,
Giving thanks to everyone
Who took a piece of my broken heart.
Cracked and broken dreams
dismembered the man inside,
However I've overcome
and hold my head with pride

GLITCH

They say a picture speaks a thousand words,

But sometimes a thousand words

paints a better picture,

I'll lay it all out there, I hope you take it with you.

And with these words I speak I'll also jot some lines,

To paint a picture just for you

with hopes you change your mind.

They speak on me the fool who never learns a lesson,

Even God has turned his back, sick of my confessions.

I've been pushing all the buttons,

Though the tracks don't want to switch,

Repeat the vicious cycle, I'm feeling like a glitch.

Questing for a purpose curiosity had me loomin',

Before I knew what hit me, Wham, I was zoomin'.

It was barely a kiss, a mere peck on the cheek,

Adrenaline surge had me up for a week.

Felt like Superman, I flew to the moon,

So unrealistic I was in a cartoon.

But it was real and I was me,

Except I was super and I felt so free.

Confidence about me I stood so tall,

Brick by brick I constructed some walls.

My fortress of solitude shot to the sky,

So proud of myself I kept getting high.

Why would I not, I felt like the man,

With the flick of a Bic, the world in my hand.

But coming down was a hell of a doozy,

Yet I was finally the director of my life's own movie.

I devoured so much food I nearly ate the cabinets,

This was only the beginning of so many bad habits.

I went down like a fainting goat, nearly slept a week,

I really had no choice, my body was so weak.

All strength seemed to evade me

as I struggled with my bed,

But that crystalline substance

was dancing in my head.

Surely just one hit I could probably be okay,

But I needed a dozen more

just to make it through the day.

After only a month my life took on a change,

Reflection in the mirror said I looked a little strange.

Darkness around my eyes, the light inside went dim,

Self-deceit bought me out

even though I was getting thin.

Months of this stacked up, calendar flipped to years,

So caught up being selfish I failed to see your tears.

But your eyes give you away,

every day I ask forgiveness,

I noticed my shoes, but who's life really is this?

Regrets bite deep, incarceration helped me see,

Everything I lost was so much more than me.

And you noticed something about me,

you said I was different,

To me it was normal and how I was livin'.

I still felt okay even though I was gone,

Your voice beckoned to me,

"please come back home".

I knew I wasn't alone but it's hard to see proof,
So I silenced your voice, afraid of the truth.
Snort another line, off like a rocket,
Anytime I saw your calls I shoved you in my pocket.
Perhaps I was afraid you wouldn't understand,
I was gone so long how could I stand
In front of you, the same old loser,
Still an addict, a junky, the worst kind of abuser.

I never thought my use could hurt you so bad,
Now so much time is gone it makes me so mad.
Truth be told it's no longer fun,
I'm sick of the rabbit holding the gun,
And me always living my life on the run.
But there's a monster on my back
and the worst kind of demon,
Been given a curse but for what is the reason?
Stopped prayin' to God, havin' troubles believin',
Still hopin' for help, I need the change of a season.
Guess I've grown accustomed to this lifestyle,
it's what I'm used to,

Remember how I used to,

Want to grow up to be just like Dad,

Still striving for that but it makes me so sad,

It took everything from me

like some kind of mobster,

You want to see my mistakes look at the roster.

They call it a narcotic but it's medicine to me,

Buries my pain, helps me feel free.

And I know you can't see my perspective,

So please look through eyes

with an empirical objective.

A drop of water given time

bores a hole through a rock,

Drugs just the same took what I got.

Material objects first to go, nothing left to sell,

That's when life sent me right back to hell.

Clutching to hope in a cold dark place,

Back in his cell, myself I would face.

All the judging and condemning people sent my way,

Is nothing compared to the things I'd say.

Destruction within, better a punch to the chin,

I chew on regrets deep down and then,

I call to you with hopes that I find,

Positive affirmation instead of this grind.

Perhaps you didn't realize I strung my own noose,

Would it help you feel better if I told you my truth?

Honestly, I don't know how to not get high,

It's embedded in me like it's part of my eye.

And I know it's hard to hear

it takes more than a knife,

But I'm not just cutting some friends out my life.

At times it's all I had like a single sun ray,

It kept me alive day after day.

When I was homeless and hopeless

it kept me all warm,

Eyes to the sky I wished to be home.

Roaming around things I thought were worth it,

Looking back now my decisions weren't perfect.

So many nights I didn't sleep,

too damn often I didn't eat,

This was my secret, I kept it discreet.

Next went my mind, my innate moral code,

Not living my virtues helped me reload,

Pipe after pipe till it no longer worked,

First needle in my arm caused me to jerk.

Sent out my mind I went all berserk,

But doing much better, the injection had worked.

Monster amplified; addiction bigger than ever,

He stayed by my side, I thought I was clever.

Before I knew it everything was gone,

My friends, my family, even my home.

Draggin' Bodies through trenches; addiction's fallout,

Buried some friends, from the graves they call out.

Suddenly I realized this is my fate,

Standing in line, why do I wait?

Just kill myself and get it over already,

But for death's final sting who's really ready.

I'm not sure what's left to say but I want to get right,

Kick this cursed habit before there's no light.

So I live for today, not tomorrow's troubles,
Hopefully by then my sobriety doubles.
Moment by moment I'm leaving this beast,
Hold the applause, there will be no feast.
Until he's behind me, so far out of sight,
You see a difference in me like day does the night.
Because I know your hearts have been tested
and sifted through a strainer,
So has my entire life, the next steps a no-brainer.

I pulled the wool over their eyes just to blind myself,
No one's meant to be alone, I'll need some help.
Your voice in hard times it calms me down,
If I go it alone, I'll surely drown.
If I look for you, would you be found?
Would you catch my tears as they fall to the ground?

It's easy to neglect people when they're not there,
Life isn't a festival and no it's not fair.
Will I get another chance,
though I've asked this before,
A glitch changed my mind and opened a door.

Windows have to like never before,

Below rocks at the bottom, you've been there before?

Everyday is a struggle with many more confessions,

I'm telling you now I've learned all the lessons.

So here's to you, and to me,

and to people in the struggle,

When life's torn apart we rebuild from the rubble,

And eliminate the garbage to kick this dumbass habit,

Because the life I'm dreaming of, I'm gonna have it,

Sincerely, truly, and always,

Your addict.

THE END